HORSE AND PONY
BODY LANGUAGE
PHRASEBOOK

HORSE AND PONY
BODY LANGUAGE
PHRASEBOOK

Susan McBane

THUNDER BAY
P·R·E·S·S

San Diego, California

Thunder Bay Press

An imprint of the Advantage Publishers Group

THUNDER BAY   10350 Barnes Canyon Road, San Diego, CA 92121
P · R · E · S · S   www.thunderbaybooks.com

Copyright © Salamander Books 2008
An imprint of Anova Books Company Ltd.

All notations of errors or omissions should be addressed to Thunder Bay Press,
Editorial Department, at the above address. All other correspondence (author
inquiries, permissions) concerning the content of this book should be addressed
to Salamander Books, 10 Southcombe Street, London W14 0RA, U.K.

Library of Congress Cataloging-in-Publication Data

McBane, Susan.
 Horse and pony body language phrasebook / Susan McBane.
    p. cm.
 Includes index.
 ISBN-13: 978-1-59223-948-1
 ISBN-10: 1-59223-948-X
 1. Horses--Behavior. 2. Ponies--Behavior. 3. Human-animal communication. I. Title.
 SF281.M3315 2008
 636.1--dc22

                          2008030192

Printed by Times Offset Sdn Bhd
1 2 3 4 5 12 11 10 09 08

Contents

Introduction

Horses have a unique position in history, and they have been more useful to humans than any other animal. They come midway between pet animals and work animals yet often fulfill the roles of both.

All the wars in our history up to the middle of the last century were driven by horsepower and the outcomes of many would have been very different if it had not been for their speed, size, strength, trainability, patience, and endurance. Not only warfare but also transportation and farmwork have depended on equines—from the smallest ponies hauling coal down mines, to carriage and draft horses carrying people, mail, and goods over hundreds of miles, to teams of massive heavy horses working the vast plains of America. Pack ponies and stock horses have enabled our civilizations to grow at a rate unimaginable without them.

The role for which horses have been mainly recognized over the last sixty years or so in the Western world has been in leisure and sport. They have been used for hunting and sport for thousands of years—polo and racing are the two oldest equestrian sports known. The burgeoning of competitive riding has exploded beyond all imagination since the end of World War II. Competition is still extremely popular—some would say excessively so—while over the last twenty or thirty years there has been a gradual increase in the number of people who want to ride for its own sake, not just to win prizes. A genuine interest in sharing time and activities with horses and wanting to look after them are the very best of reasons to want a horse of your own.

Horses are big animals, among the biggest on the planet, but, as mammals, they are fairly closely related to us. The well-known saying "as strong as a horse" was coined for a reason—even a small pony can drag a large man around with little effort if it wants to. But they can

Knowing the factors that could affect a horse's temperament is important for young riders.

also be gentle and highly sensitive animals who enjoy company. If well treated, they are happy to be around humans and to cooperate with them. Most horses feel vulnerable or even frightened without other horses around, and act accordingly.

They are also labor-intensive to look after in most domestic situations, needing feeding, grooming, exercising, schooling, shoeing, and cleaning. They may also need to be fitted with expensive equipment like saddles, bridles, rugs, and blankets, and sometimes even require their own transport vehicles. Managing them can be simplified by letting them live freely out

Horses are most confident and happy in groups, especially when allowed to roam freely.

of doors, in pastures, fields, and paddocks, but, even here, they need watching to ensure that they have everything they need—food, water, shelter, and company—and are settled and thriving.

There is no getting away from it: to keep horses decently takes time, effort, commitment, and money. We have to accept responsibility for the horse's welfare, which means that we have to understand them. That, in turn, means that we have to be willing to learn as much as we can about them.

This book has been written for first-time horse owners and people who may not have their own horse but ride at a riding school or center and have little knowledge or experience with them. It is

specifically about learning to understand the signals they use—mainly their body language—which helps us interpret their feelings and intentions.

Most recently, in evolutionary terms, horses evolved as highly specialized grazing, running prey animals on wide-open grassy plains in America, then Asia and Europe. They are among the fastest land animals on earth. At first thought, it may seem that they are fairly defenseless against predators with sharp claws and flesh-tearing and bone-crushing teeth. Horses have neither of these, nor do they have horns—but they have a kick that can kill a lioness or severely disable her, and a bite that can easily disembowel another large animal, let alone break the spine of a hunting dog or cat.

Clearly, horses are potentially dangerous, but if they are trained properly, ridden or driven with some acquired skill, and treated well, they are safe and rewarding companions. They do not want to fight unless they are trapped. It is important for us to realize this, and its effects are explained in the first section, on evolution.

The body language horses developed to communicate with each other is the same language they use with other animals and humans. It is therefore important that we learn to understand their body language because not knowing what a horse is thinking, feeling, and intending to do can cause confusion for both parties, and can also be dangerous.

To people who are used to interacting with dogs and cats as friends and companions, horse behavior can seem strange. They are not hunters like dogs and cats, but find their food in nature. This calls for a very different approach, one based on self-defense rather than hunting, with a mind that is easily startled and that becomes suspicious with anything new, unusual, or different.

This outlook on life is common to all equines, including all the hundreds of breeds and types that people have created from the few wild, evolutionary types existing 6,000 years ago, when the horse first started to be domesticated. It colors our understanding of equine behavior and how we should behave around horses.

Fortunately, horses and ponies give clear physical signs of how they are feeling and what they are intending to do. Learning to understand and interpret their body language, and combining this with a grasp of their natural equine outlook on life, will mean that we can understand them most of the time and act accordingly.

"This is where I belong."

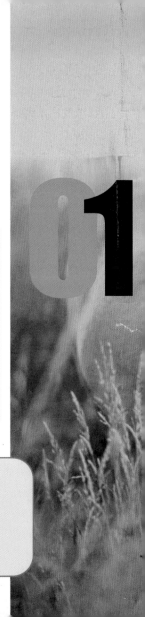

At first, horse predecessors were small, multitoed forest and swamp dwellers that lived on the leaves of plants, trees, and bushes. As the earth's climate changed, various grasses evolved and began to grow on drier, open plains—and those equine forerunners that adapted to cope with these changes populated the plains. The primitive horses grew bigger, developing longer legs and reducing their toes to just one—an extreme running speciality found only in horses, asses, and zebras. Their necks and heads elongated so that they could easily reach down to the grass, and their teeth became bigger, stronger, and specialized to crop off and grind up the tough grasses.

THE AGE OF THE HORSE

The first single-toed grazers appeared about 4 million years ago and developed the instincts we are familiar with in modern equines. The equine species we know—horses, asses, etc.—emerged about a million years ago.

"We love the wide-open spaces."

Early horses learned that galloping away in a group was their best chance of escaping predators (which were also evolving to catch this bigger, faster food source). There were no trees to hinder their progress, and horses developed a psychological preference to be in spacious surroundings with a good view of the area—a preference that is still present in them today.

"We can't get enough of this."

The main food of horses in nature is grass. Horses are foragers, which means that they seek their food wherever they can find it. Grass is their favorite, followed by leaves from shrubs and trees, and also roots scraped out of the ground. This vegetarian diet is tough to eat, so horses have very strong, specialized teeth. Incisors, or front teeth, crop off grass very close to the ground if necessary, so they can cope with very short "keep" (food supplies) with cheek teeth (premolars and molars) at the backs of their mouths with very hard, grinding surfaces to break up the tough grass and mix it with saliva before swallowing it. Most of the year, grass is not very nutritious, and horses have evolved to live on a lot of poor-quality grass. To take in enough nourishment, they have developed a pattern of eating for about two-thirds of their day.

HE'S NOT GREEDY

Well, some horses might be greedy, but most eat at every opportunity because that's how nature has made them. It must be very difficult for them to go out on a hack with lots of juicy grass and leaves around, and have their owner stop them from eating it when their instincts are telling them the very opposite!

"I'm faster off the blocks than a car!"

Horses in the open have nowhere to hide from potential predators, so they have two means of evading capture and becoming someone's dinner: they gallop off like lightning when startled by anything they believe could be a predator, or they try to stay close to the herd and blend in so that it is difficult for a predator to pick out just one horse. Any horse that is slow to get away could be sick or injured, and therefore easier to catch. If something startles a domestic herd in a field, such as marauding wolves, they can accidentally run into fences, trees, or other objects and injure themselves. In the wild, horses are not equipped to cope with obstructions like these.

05

"Look out!
I'm coming through!"

Healthy horses can go from 0 to 40 miles per hour in under five seconds, which is faster than a typical family car. This is their speciality, and you don't want to be in their way when they're doing it. Although they set off like lightning and keep up a fast gallop for several minutes, their attention is behind them on whatever they are running away from, so it is not safe to be in front of a galloping herd.

"Is someone talking about me?"

Horses have very acute hearing and can hear sounds from farther away, and at a higher pitch, than humans can. Their sense of hearing is one of their protective mechanisms against danger. Horses can easily hear an animal making a rustling sound in the grass nearby, which tells them that a predator has come too close. A horse's outer ear, the part we can see on the top and to the sides of its head, is called the pinna. Its funnel shape—plus the fact that each ear can, independently, turn a 180-degree half circle, from facing frontward to facing backward—means that the horse can pick up sounds from all around.

SPEAK TO ME CAREFULLY!

Horses are very susceptible to the sound and tone of the human voice, which is a valuable aid in daily care and training.

"I can't believe my ears!"

Some horses become nervous on windy days, so much that many owners will not ride in windy conditions. This is because the wind itself is noisy, and also distorts both the nature of the sounds the horse can hear, but also the direction the sounds are coming from. So the horse is unsure what the noise could be or where the potential danger is coming from. This can be unsettling and even frightening for him, although many horses become calmer with time and a human they trust.

"That must be a lion behind that hedge!"

Horses' eyesight is probably the sense that is most different from ours. Their sight is geared to spotting movement (predators) rather than sharp detail or full color, although they are not color-blind. Their eyes are set to the sides of their heads, which gives them close to 360-degree vision—a tremendous advantage for a prey animal. A horse sees different views with each eye, known as monocular vision, but can also focus both eyes at once on objects directly in front, known as binocular vision. He can see directly behind him if he just turns his head slightly to one side, but has a blind spot for about four feet directly in front of him in a downward direction. The lens in his eye cannot change shape easily to focus in the way that a human's can, so he moves his head around to direct the image entering his eye onto the retina at the back of his eye—up and out for distant objects, in and down for close objects. He has a narrow, horizontal strip of fairly acute vision running across the back of the retina, unlike our round area, with less-sharp vision above and below it. His vision, therefore, is perfect for his natural life but can cause him to be easily spooked.

"Hmm, that smells good enough to eat."

The horse's sense of smell is his second line of investigation when checking out food and other items. First, he will use his vision. Then he will smell something, and if it smells like food, he will taste it. It has been said that if the membrane inside the horse's nasal passages were spread out on the ground, it would cover an area as big as a soccer field. Horses certainly use their sense of smell a great deal, and it is said to be almost as good as that of a dog. They are interested in smelling most things, not just food, and, like most animals, experience a wide world of scents almost completely unknown to us. They can pick up smells on the wind, and a stallion can smell a mare in season up to a mile away if the wind is blowing in the right direction.

"This requires further analysis."

Sometimes you can see a horse raising his muzzle in an action known as the flehmen response. He is turning up his top lip and showing his teeth to use the Jacobson's organ in his nasal passages; this organ is used to analyze each scent. The action of curling up his top lip (which may be the source of the expression "turning his nose up") partly closes the nostrils and allows the smell to be assessed by the sensitive Jacobson's organ.

"Grass: it does the body good."

Horses vary widely in their attitudes toward eating. Some are apparent gluttons, eating anything and everything in sight, while others are extremely finicky and drive their owners crazy in the search for a feed they will eat. However, one thing is fairly certain: all horses love grass. As horses evolved on it, this is not surprising. Taste buds cover not only horses' tongues but also the upper throat areas. Horses can taste sweet, sour, salty, and bitter flavors. Many people believe that horses have a sweet tooth—and a lot of horses do enjoy molasses, honey, and sweets. They also enjoy savory flavors, and feral horses will travel many miles to salt deposits to obtain this essential mineral. Because most poisonous plants taste bitter, they avoid them, unless they are extremely hungry or have somehow acquired a taste for them.

NO CALORIE COUNTING HERE.

It seems that horses choose their food solely on taste and texture, generally preferring moist food to dry. Unlike people, horses appear to have no sense of the caloric or nutritional content of their food.

"Hey, we're sensitive, too."

Like humans, horses can feel by means of nerve endings in their skin, which detect pressure, pain, heat, and cold. Although they have no nerve endings in the parts of their bodies considered "horny"—in places like their hooves, which are modified skin cells like our fingernails—the feet are sensitive inside and can sense pressure, pain, and probably heat and cold. It is the horse's sense of touch that enables him to work with a rider's aids or signals. They can sense very light aids and, if they are well-schooled, there is no need for anything stronger. If a horse does not respond to firmer aids, it is usually because he does not understand, or just cannot do what is asked of him, either because of pain or undue difficulty.

"Tiny tortures!"

Horses can feel a tiny fly land on their skin. In fact, horses can become extremely upset by the irritation of flies and should therefore be protected from them in the summer months by using a shelter, fly repellents, or lightweight, insect-proof clothing. They show their distress by constantly nodding their heads, rubbing their skin, stamping their feet, and swishing their tails. Two horses will often stand in the shade side by side, flicking the flies away from each other's face with their tails.

"Oh, no!
I'm home alone!"

Both dogs and horses are social animals, but whereas dogs can become accustomed to being the only animal in a family of humans, horses almost always cannot. The majority of them feel insecure when alone, and their stress levels rise. Even when around humans they trust, they are never as content as they are with other horses. The solitary horse may begin refusing to work without another horse present. Or he might refuse to leave the stables, spend the whole ride calling out for others, rush to get back when you turn for home, and may even behave "badly" by throwing his head around, refusing to walk when asked, half-rearing, and so on. Youngsters should at first be handled and taught with others nearby, but should not be ridden out alone until they are well established in obeying humans, and confident enough to work alone on their home premises.

SECOND BEST

The best company for a horse or pony is another horse or pony. Some people provide donkeys, goats, sheep, or cattle, which is better than nothing, but certainly second best. Most horses have to work alone (with humans) at least some of the time, so this is an important part of schooling.

"After you; I insist."

A horse will show his nervousness about going ahead, or passing something that he deems scary by becoming tense and stiff, holding his head high, putting on the brakes, and disobeying his rider's signals. He may snort in fear or try to obtain the scent of the thing he does not want to pass. Whipping and spurring the horse, shouting at him, and generally getting rough usually makes the horse more afraid. It convinces him that there *is*, in fact, something to fear, and the emotional distress (and possibly pain) he experiences from this treatment adds to his conviction and bad memories. A traditional and useful way of using the herd instinct to your advantage is to get an experienced and reliable horse to go first and allow a more hesitant one—whether a youngster or inexperienced older horse—to follow his lead, being sure to praise him profusely as he goes.

"I want to play with my friends."

Many owners complain that their horses are too attached to their equine companions, not wanting to leave them to come in from the field or go out to work. Their evolution has made them feel safe and secure in a group. Natural groups tend to be no more than about twelve individuals, mainly family members, but strong bonding also occurs between smaller groups and pairs. From a human's viewpoint, horses who won't leave others seem like a real nuisance, but the main message coming from this is that the horse feels safer with his companions than with his handler or rider. Cultivating a calm but kind, no-nonsense attitude helps with training, as does gradually separating the horse from his companions for longer periods. Gradually, he should realize that they are always reunited and that you are a safe, fun human to be with, and will transfer some of his need for security to you.

EMERGENCY TACTICS

In the wild, equine family groups often join together in one big herd when danger threatens in order to reduce the chances of being caught. Predators are normally satisfied with one kill at a time, so the more there are in the herd, the less chance there is of that kill being a single horse, for example.

"Here comes trouble."

Horses usually feel that there is safety in numbers, preferably with others they know, either their families or other nonaggressive horses. Feral horses—and also wild zebras and asses—bunch together when being chased by predators and seem to try to get into the middle of the herd. This is because predators often surround it and pick off those around the edges. Even predators that attack from a high vantage point, such as leopards and mountain lions, will try to choose a lone animal, as it will be easier to kill without the confusion of others milling around. Domestic horses in a field will gather together when something approaches, which they see as dangerous—even a human coming to bring them in. They will look toward you at first, heads high and ears pointed toward you. Then, if you continue to approach and are obviously intent on catching one of them, they might start moving around. Horses who trust their attendants often come to be caught willingly.

TIDBITS

If you go into a herd carrying tidbits in your pockets, be prepared to be mugged! It can be pretty dangerous if they squabble over you, so try to always catch horses without carrying any food with you.

8

"We're like birds of a feather—except with more legs."

Horses' coat colors are an indirect part of their body language, yet an important safety feature in nature that horses seem to understand almost subconsciously. Prehistoric colors were probably buckskin, dun, and various browns, as these blend in best with the environment of shrubs, trees, shade patterns on the ground, earth colors, and a forest environment. Modern horses have evolved other colors that would not help at all in the wild—such as white (including the pale gray of old horses), which would stand out to predators a mile away, and similarly palomino, black, and, some argue, sorrel and chestnut. Horses often prefer to be with horses of their own or similar colors regardless of age, sex, or breed.

"They can't see the wood for the horses."

It is thought that spotted patterns are an ancient trait, and a continuation from when horse ancestors were forest animals, and striped or dappled patterns helped them blend in with their habitat. Zebras might seem to call attention to themselves, but a herd of stripes mingling and running together is extremely confusing to canine or feline predators, which have limited color vision.

"It's my turn for guard duty."

In natural conditions or when they are out together in a paddock, groups of horses take turns acting as guards for the others. Large herds (of twelve or more) will have more than one horse on duty at any one time. Watch a herd in a pasture, or a feral one if you can, and notice that they will graze calmly, interact with each other, and play, and then one or two will lie down. Others will follow, and one or more will remain standing, either grazing or just loafing, but highly alert. After half an hour or so, one of the guards will lie down and another one or two will get to their feet and graze for a while or stand around looking about them, calm but alert.

IT'S JUST WHAT HORSES DO

You can see sentinel behavior even in horses stabled individually in a barn or yard. Some will be lying down and resting while one, two, or more will be standing, sometimes alert and eating their hay or with their heads out over their doors. It is thought to be a remnant of wild behavior, when a watch had to be kept at all times for the approach of predators or unfamiliar horses.

21

"Don't rush up to me. I'm thinking."

It is inconsiderate and possibly dangerous to quickly approach a horse lying down, when he feels his most vulnerable. He could jump to his feet and knock you over. Always take it slowly, and speak to him as well.

"Don't mess with me!"

Although the idea of a herd of horses having one leader or boss has been found to be false, they do have a kind of ranking system. A common expression for this has been "herd hierarchy," but this does not accurately represent the situation, as there is no strict hierarchical order as such from top to bottom. As with other animals and humans, some individuals have a natural air of authority or self-confidence about them. This is not a bullying nature—which is usually the result of insecurity or uncertainty—but an aura of self-containment and, in mares, grace, which places them above others and which those others, in turn, understand and defer to. A high-ranking horse will not need to exert its authority much at all. Just a look is enough to move others out of the way, off the best grazing, out of the shelter, or away from a friend. This does not mean that such horses habitually order others about. They are often patient and tolerant. But if another horse, usually an up-and-coming youngster or newcomer, really challenges them, the higher-ranking horse goes into action with teeth and feet and quells any uprising in no uncertain terms.

"You're invading my personal space!"

Horses are fussy about whom they let into close proximity to them. In nature, they have no need to put up with being around horses they do not like, or those they fear. In domesticity, however, they often have no choice, which can be very stressful for them. Just imagine how you would feel in this situation. It is believed that horses have a personal space of roughly 25 feet around their bodies, which is clearly much larger than the average stable. This means that, even in his stable, a horse can be upset by a "non-preferred" neighbor. This can show by means of a tense body and face, kicking the stable walls, nodding the head, restlessness, poor appetite, not looking over the stable door, and, sometimes, being afraid to enter or exit the stable. In the same way, it is considerate and wise never to rush up to a horse—and into its personal space—but to speak his name, look at him softly, and let him smell you if he wishes.

"No, I'm not pleased to see you."

Although not exactly ritualized, greetings among horses follow a common procedure. They will approach each other, ears pricked, and enter the other's personal space, which can be a domineering gesture depending on how it is done. They visually assess the other horse's identity and mood, then they sniff each other's breath, nostril to nostril, one at a time, and often their whole bodies. If the horses already know one another, it may end there. With strange horses, this is often accompanied by quiet or loud squeals, and the more superior of the two may stamp or actually strike out with a foreleg. This is largely the act of a stallion, but some geldings do it and high-ranking mares might, too. If the most assertive decides that he is not keen on the other, his ears may go back and he may deliver a nip or threaten to do so. If the other one decides the same thing, or takes the hint, he will move away and it all ends there. If a mare decides she does not want to be near another horse who will not go away, she may turn tail and kick out with one or both hind feet.

"I'm warning you . . ."

Striking out with a front leg can be done as fast as lightning and with no regard for nearby humans who may be caught in the cross fire. This act may be part of the introduction process between strange horses, but it can also occur between those who know each other and who are having a difference of opinion, possibly field mates who are not the best of friends. Striking out takes place early on in situations that are probably going to turn into fights, and it is mainly stallions who do it, although geldings can do so as well. As it is usually done in a head-on body posture, it is dangerous and bones can be broken by a strike from a shod horse. When riding out with strange horses—although this is a good way to introduce them safely—it is wise not to let them get head-on. Keep them side by side, if close, and keep them moving so that there can be no striking. Stallions may be perfectly safe to ride out and work together if common sense is used, and whole stables always work together in racing yards.

"I said keep away from my new coat!"

Kicking with the hind feet is a form of self-defense, particularly in mares. It's a sign of frustration and also a challenge. Horses may kick with only one leg or, when sufficiently emotionally aroused, with both (commonly known as "both barrels"). In a challenge situation, a horse will usually look at what he wants to kick in order to gauge his aim. His ears will be back and he will normally have a sour expression on his face, probably with nostrils wrinkled up and back. He will raise his tail slightly, raise the leg he is going to use, and then kick backward quickly. Horses with abdominal pain, known as colic, often kick forward and up toward their bellies, where the pain is. They often look anxious or even angry, with ears back and a distressed facial expression. These are symptoms that should concern you because colic can be agonizing and even fatal.

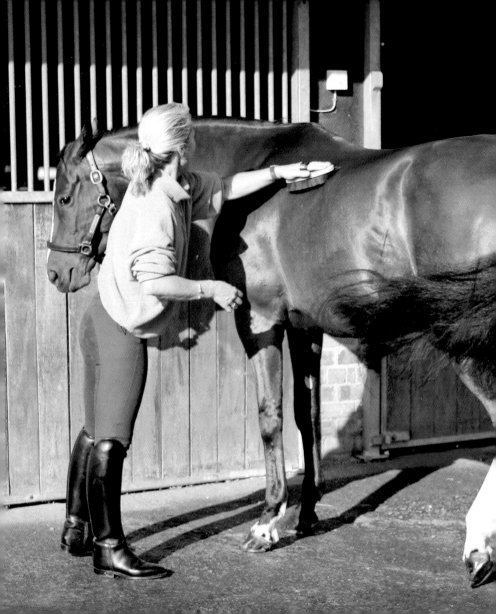

"Wherever you go, I can get you."

Horses can kick backward, forward, and sideways (called "cow-kicking") with their hind legs, so you really have to be careful, particularly around horses you do not know. Always face the hind legs with such horses and keep your distance as much as you can. If the horse is so problematic that you cannot groom or handle the hind legs, and the horse cannot have his hind feet attended to, seek expert help from a behavioral therapist, as such horses are too dangerous for novices.

"I'm warning you, I mean business."

A meaningful bite from a horse can cause painful and serious injury to another horse or animal, or to a human. Biting is mainly a form of self-defense but it is also used aggressively by some horses. Horses use their front incisor teeth to bite, and these teeth are a formidable weapon capable of tearing flesh and inflicting fatal injuries. Horses planning to bite use the angry facial expression—ears pressed hard and flat back against the top of the neck, an angry look in the eyes, nostrils wrinkled up and back, the head and neck outstretched toward the target, the mouth open, and teeth bared.

29

"Hey, not too tight!"

If the biting is used on humans, experienced help (not abuse) from a behavioral therapist will be needed to extinguish it, as it is probably based on the memory of pain inflicted by humans, maybe during just one unpleasant or painful procedure. Girthing up is a very common trigger, as many people do it roughly, carelessly, and quickly.

SAFETY FIRST

Dealing with a biter is no task for a novice horse person. Do not think that by being nice to him he will not bite you. Also do not think that by hitting him when he bites you he will stop: the reverse is the case. You are a human and he associates humans with pain. Get expert help.

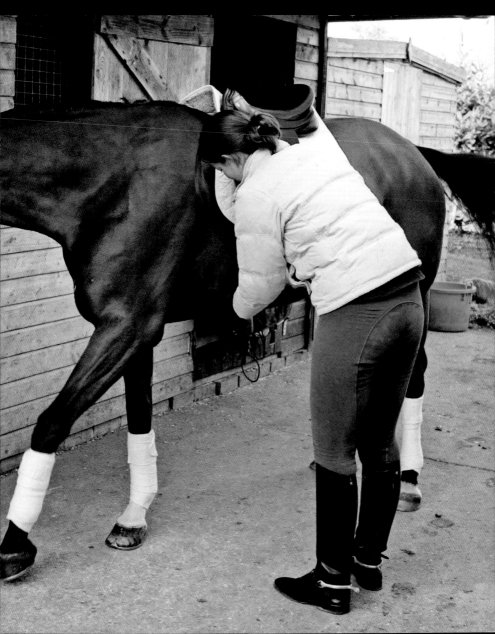

"Let's just sort out this messy hair."

Nipping—a kind of a mini bite—occurs during play fighting, aggression, courting, and, more softly, during mutual grooming. It is used by horses who mug us for food, usually tidbits. A nip should, in the horse's eyes, stimulate the hand that feeds him. Hitting and vocally reprimanding the horse does not stop nipping, but instant discomfort, seen as self-inflicted, can work. First be absolutely sure that his nipping is not the result of pain and suffering. Have something moderately prickly in your hand and, as he turns to nip you, place it between yourself and his teeth so that it pricks his muzzle. Do not look at him or speak, as he will then associate the unpleasantness with you. Just carry on as normal. He will soon link the pricking with nipping and should stop it.

A GOLDEN RULE

If you have a horse who shows that he will readily nip for food, your simplest solution is to make it an absolute rule that you never give tidbits to him or, to be fair, any horse within his view. He will learn quickly that he does not now get tidbits no matter what happened in his previous home, and the behavior should stop in due course.

"Take you to our leader? What's a leader?"

Many mammals, including humans, live in groups with one leader: we find this social organization easy to understand and so tend to see it where it does not actually exist. The image of a stallion leading his harem over the grassy plains is one such glamorous but erroneous myth that is difficult for us to relinquish. Modern behavioral researchers and observers have proven it to be a myth. Although apparent dominance interactions can be seen by anyone watching almost any group of horses or ponies, careful observation and assessment have shown that there is no "top horse" or "herd boss" in all situations. Horses like to live as a cohesive group, in small herds of up to about a dozen, but often less, so long as life is peaceful. If two or more herds live close by, they often merge when danger threatens, going their own way again when peace is restored. This behavior can also be seen in a large domestic field, where separate groups of two or more friends may graze peacefully, all coming together if something threatening occurs.

"I really don't want to fight, but I will if you force me."

Horses are generally peace-loving animals. All they really want to do is socialize happily with their herd, eat as much as they need, drink, find shelter, and be free. Sound familiar? If trouble presents itself, such as a predator or an aggressive horse causing trouble, most horses will want to get out of the way, which can result in a headlong gallop if it is a predator, or just cantering a short distance away if it is something less extreme. They fight only if pushed to it by being trapped (such as being tied up or cornered in a stable or field) or because another horse will not leave them alone. The latter circumstance may arise in the wild if a strange stallion tries to take over the herd and challenges the existing herd stallion, when there can be a fight to the death if neither backs down. A hostile or challenging horse will draw himself up, prick his ears, and arch his neck and tail. He will stamp and snort and circle his opponent, who may adopt the same posture while they assess each other. If the "victim" does not fancy his chances, he may lower his neck, head, and tail a little, put his ears back, turn his tail to his enemy, and maybe kick out in defense—or just run away.

"Hmm, she smells quite interesting."

Feral stallions' normal tenure of a herd of mares is roughly four years, while they are at the peak of their powers. A stallion will try to find his own herd by looking for stray mares and fillies, stealing them from another herd, or challenging an existing stallion for his herd, particularly one who is injured, sick, old, or clearly past his prime. When the previous stallion's foals are born, the new one may try to kill them. As horses breed seasonally—in spring—this cannot be because he wants to impregnate the dams again quickly, because they will soon come into season anyway. Opinions vary as to why this happens, but it may simply be that the new stallion does not want the previous stallion's foals (i.e., his genes) to survive, particularly males, and foals are easy to get rid of.

34

"We ladies are the family foundation."

The long-term nucleus of the herd is mainly related females with their offspring of various ages. Sexually mature colts pose a threat to a stallion and he usually kicks them out of the herd. It has been reported that some stallions may kick out their own daughters as a natural control on inbreeding and its dangers, although this seems rare.

"I'm not the boss; I'm just a keen herder."

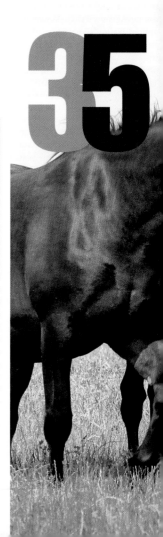

Stallions can be seen herding their mares and their youngsters around in the typical stallion herding behavior of moving their neck and head down and out, snaking from side to side with ears back, and with an "I mean it" look in his eyes—and maybe with teeth showing. This has given rise to the belief that the stallion is the big boss and everyone does as he says. In fact, this herding behavior occurs mainly to keep the herd together in the face of danger from either a predator or an opportunistic stallion trying to take over, or even a young, sexually mature male herd member trying to mate the odd mare on the sly. The herd stallion will then place himself between the herd and the "problem" and will stand his ground, squaring up for a fight if necessary. As for his being the boss in other circumstances, this does not happen. As mentioned previously, horses do not have conventional bosses. The stallion just lives with the mares peaceably, being friendly toward them when not in season, and also associating with his foals like a good dad. It is amazing what liberties some stallions will stand for from their foals!

36

"Let's follow her. She seems to know what she's doing."

Another myth, more recently dispelled, is that the real boss of the herd is a matriarchal mare, a "lead mare" who keeps the others in order. It is true that horse society seems to be mainly matriarchal and that mares form strong bonds with their filly foals, but it is likely that if the colts were also allowed to stay in the herd, they would form just as strong bonds with their dams. The impression of a "lead mare" may have come about because an experienced, mature mare may acquire so much knowledge that she knows what to do in any circumstance, and the others may be reassured by her confident attitude, so they are glad to follow her example. Such a mare will not encourage others to go with her, except for her own foal if she has one. She will simply go to a particular spot, start doing something (such as loafing in the shade, grazing, or rolling), and the others follow suit because they like to do things communally.

"Not going anywhere, any time soon."

When researchers and students study how horses spend their time in different circumstances, they usually find that horses do not particularly exert themselves (other than youngsters playing) any more than necessary. Even so, a feral herd can easily cover twenty-five miles a day in its wanderings to find grazing, shelter, and water—and its members will be very fit.

"The colts are back in town."

You may wonder what happens to all those colts who are kicked out of the herd by the stallion. The answer is that they all hang together in what are termed "bachelor bands." A lone horse is at great risk of predation in the wild and will not normally last long. So, once again, there is greater safety in numbers. Bachelor bands may consist of young colts, older ones who have not yet managed to form a herd of females of their own, and also older, defeated stallions who have not been able to conquer a reigning herd stallion to acquire his breeding rights.

39

"Hey, Iaaady!"

In domestic circumstances, stallions are normally kept stabled on studs or in competition yards. They are popular for dressage and endurance events, and they are also kept in racing stables, where they can be strictly controlled and managed. They may be turned out alone or with a suitable pony for a relatively short time on most days. This may well be because there are also mares on the yard who come into season and naturally unsettle the stallions. In such a situation, turning out stallions together would almost certainly result in serious injury or death. In feral bachelor bands, however, there are no mares around and therefore nothing to fight over, so peace normally reigns.

"It's all good."

If we accept that horse society does not work on the basis of a herd boss, how do we account for those signs of respect and submission that often pass between horses? It has not been scientifically proven that horses have what we understand as "respect" for each other—acknowledgment of another's deeds or position. However, we can clearly see what we take as submission being declared. The most obvious case of apparent submission being shown is in youngsters, particularly foals to older horses, and sometimes to humans or other animals. The youngster will open and close its front teeth quickly in a motion called "snapping" or sometimes "clapping." His or her neck will be outstretched, the muzzle out, and there will be a soft, inquiring look in the eyes. The ears may be anywhere from forward to back, depending on what the youngster thinks are its chances of being accepted. Snapping can be taken to mean, generally, "I'm no threat to you and have no intention of hurting you. Please don't harm me." Behavioral experts do not feel that it means anything like "I accept you as superior to me and I accept your senior position."

41

"I'm uncomfortable with this."

The mouthing action known as "licking and chewing" has come to be widely accepted by the lay horse public as meaning that a horse is submissive. Some people use training methods that involve chasing a horse away from them, then letting him approach, then sending him away again, which many feel causes stress and confusion. After a while of this, most horses will lick and chew. Licking and chewing is seen by some behavioral experts as a sign of distress, not submission. A dry mouth indicates fear in mammals, and some people think that the licking and chewing action might stimulate the production of saliva to restore comfort in the mouth.

"Go away! Right now!"

Lucy Rees, author of the classic *The Horse's Mind*, says that a horse can tell another horse to do only one thing, and that is to go away. They do this by making it unpleasant for the other horse to stick around, normally by nipping it fairly hard with their front teeth. This will be accompanied by having his ears back, a cross or angry look in the eyes, nostrils wrinkled up and back (a sign of dislike), and his head and neck lowered with his muzzle poking outward. The tail may be thrashing, too. Few horses ignore this but, if they do, the one giving the order may turn and kick out hard with both hind feet. The rejected horse will usually turn away and vacate the area immediately. He may look a little scared (ears back toward the other horse, eyes wide, head and neck up and tense, tail clamped between the buttocks), or may be cross at the liberty, making a face similar to his opponent, wheeling around and doing the same to him.

MARES AND FOALS

At times, a mare may wish to take her foal with her to another spot, but he may be busy playing with friends. She has no hands and arms to pick him up, so will herd him (again, the "go away" message) in front of her, with or without the painful nips.

43

"The sisterhood."

Just as there are bachelor bands in the wild, so herds of females may be left alone if their stallion dies or is preyed upon. A moving story was reported years ago of a herd stallion being fatally injured in a fall. His females stayed with him, as a mare will stay with her dead foal for a while, until predators put him out of his misery. When fillies are evicted from their herd, they are in the same situation as bachelors but do not seem to form "spinster bands" in quite the same way as do males. If one or more fillies try to join a bachelor band, though, it is often permitted, but it means that the most able of the males may leave his buddies and settle down to married life, and often not without serious fighting among previous good companions.

"We're all good friends."

Many stables now separate the sexes for grazing and turnout in livery yards, as it is felt by some that mixing geldings and mares together encourages fighting. In a fairly long life with horses, I have never known this to happen significantly in an established, domestic herd due to sexual differences. Skirmishes can occur between animals of either sex, and, most common where too many horses are put into one paddock, and they appear to feel crowded and stressed. The safest way—and good management practice—is to turn friends out together as they would be in the wild, regardless of sex, and to keep actual enemies well apart.

"I love fields in the springtime!"

Once the days start lengthening after the winter solstice, horses' brains register the increased daylight coming in, which brings both feral and domestic horses—including geldings—into breeding condition. Breeding hormones start circulating and cycling, and horses may start showing "silly" behavior, like squealing and frolicking, being more sensitive, and often paying less attention to humans. Over the next few months, as the weather warms, winter coats gradually cast (molt), summer coats grow, and mares start coming into season (estrus). Foals are born naturally in spring and summer to take advantage of the young, growing grass, although they often arrive earlier on domestic stud farms to encourage early maturity.

CLIMATE CHANGE

Mating and foaling take place throughout spring and summer, but climate change is causing grass to grow for longer, and for temperatures to be less predictable. Horses on and around the equator breed year-round because of stable light and temperature levels, so maybe we can expect horses to extend their natural breeding seasons in the future.

"We can't help it."

Hormones control horses' breeding activities, and their effects are irresistible. Increasing light enters the pupil of the eye and messages pass down the optic nerve to the pineal body in the brain, which reduces its release of melatonin, a breeding suppressant. Other parts of the brain react by triggering a complex program of hormonal control of the breeding cycle in stallions and mares, which gradually reverts after the summer solstice, therefore creating an annual cycle.

"Ahh, memories."

About three-quarters of geldings (castrated males) retain some stallion characteristics. This is more likely if they were gelded later than usual, which can be any time that both testicles are down, in foalhood or, more often, when the colt is a yearling to two or three years old. Production of the male hormone testosterone decreases greatly but does not cease, and can stimulate stallionlike behavior. If the horse was used as a stud before being gelded, his memories will remain and his stallion characteristics will be stronger. Such fairly rare horses, in a field of mixed sexes, may even create two herds—mares in one place and geldings in the other. Occasionally, some of these horses may mount the mares and even serve them, but they cannot ejaculate, of course.

DOES IT MATTER?

Provided these horses are turned out with their preferred friends—mares and/or geldings—there is normally no harm done. In the unlikely event of there being two such geldings on one yard, it would be best not to turn them out together with other horses during the spring and summer.

"Surprise!"

Male horses who appear to be geldings but who retain one or both testicles up in the abdomen are called cryptorchids or, colloquially, "rigs." They behave just like stallions and can sometimes get mares in foal. The testicles are usually in the scrotum (the skin sac that holds them between the hind legs) and outside the body at birth or soon afterward. They rise up into the abdomen again, but if one or both remain up after an age when the colt should have reached puberty (around three years or earlier), he is then called a rig and may be mistaken for a gelding. Healthy sperm depend on being cooler than the body temperature, so when up inside the abdomen they should, in theory, be nonviable, but many mares have been impregnated by rigs.

WHAT TO DO ABOUT IT

A veterinarian can have a blood test done to check the status of circulating hormones in suspect horses. Then owners may have a choice of chemical castration or an operation to remove the testicles up inside the abdomen. Rigs are often very frustrated animals, potentially dangerous, and often receive harsh treatment from unknowledgeable humans. Therefore, it is best for all concerned to have the situation dealt with.

"I'm in the mood for love!"

Owners of female riding horses can be quite upset or irritated by their mares' changed behavior during their seasons, particularly if it is pronounced, and this is why fewer mares compete in some disciplines than geldings. Mares in season may become overly affectionate toward humans and other animals, rubbing them, following them around, and making "cow eyes" at them. Others, maybe with a hormonal imbalance, can become more aggressive, calling out a lot, being difficult to handle, squealing, resenting work, and trying to reach male horses all the time. Some will not like having their genitals handled and cleaned, but others will not mind. Practical help from owners includes being understanding with their mares, keeping them away from others likely to hassle them, but otherwise allowing them to mix normally with their friends of either sex.

KEEPING A LID ON IT

Herbal feed additives can help mildly affected mares. Medication from a veterinarian can prevent mares from coming into season, if this is necessary or advised, and in extreme cases a veterinarian may perform an operation to remove the ovaries.

"Meet my new brother."

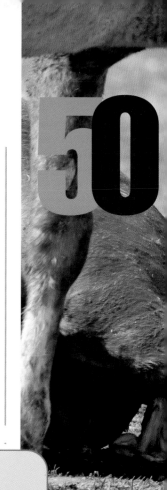

In natural conditions, spring is the time when a mare's new foal is born and the previous year's offspring has a new status. By this time, he or she will have no need for milk but may take the odd little comforting and harmless suckle—if the dam allows. She will have weaned him naturally and very slowly, and her milk will have more or less dried up around the fall. Her milk supply returns in full just before her new foal is born, to give it the benefit of "first milk," or colostrum containing protective antibodies. The older foal, now a weanling, will stay in the family but will have a much more independent life, grazing and interacting with the other herd members. In domesticity, foals are often weaned too young (roughly six months of age) and too suddenly, which some experts believe can cause extreme distress to mare and foal, sometimes leaving permanent psychological damage leading to learning difficulties, stereotypical behavior (known as "vices"), and other behavioral and physical problems later in life.

A BETTER WAY TO WEAN

Later and more gradual artificial weaning, if necessary at all, is quite practicable in domestic breeding, if breeders have the patience. It is much more humane and avoids all the problems associated with the traditional methods and timing.

"So, what are you doing tonight?"

Courtship starts in spring as the horses' reproductive instincts become stronger. Usually, an in-season mare will approach a stallion. They meet head-to-head and touch nostrils, exchanging breath, then she will swing her hindquarters toward him. He will sniff and lick her genitals, and they will spend time together. Then she may change her mind and become resistant to him, kicking out, squealing, and going away. As her season progresses, the stallion approaches the mare more often and sniffs and licks her (known as "teasing") to ascertain whether she is ready to mate. If not, she will show resistance again, but if she is ready, she will stand for him and mating takes place.

"I'm ready if you are."

Recent studies confirm that it is the mare who usually
initiates courtship as her hormones increase her desire.
As things progress, the stallion approaches her as well.
Courtship takes time because it is important for the
mare to be fully ready—around the time of ovulation—
before the stallion mounts. Otherwise, he wastes
valuable energy and risks being injured by the mare.
If she seems ready, the stallion licks the mare at her
head, continuing down her body to her genitals. Her
scent is also a guide, and the stallion uses his sense of
smell, including performing the flehmen response, as
described earlier, to assess her readiness.

"Makin' whoopee!"

When both mare and stallion are ready to mate, the stallion will mount her, sometimes from the side to reduce the chance of a kick, and then move around behind her. Often he does not have an erection at this point, in case she suddenly refuses him. When he mounts with an erection, the stallion gets close up behind the mare and actual mating takes place quickly. Again, this is due to horses being prey animals. During mating, they are vulnerable to attack. It takes the stallion several seconds to achieve ejaculation, the main signs of which are "flagging" of the tail up and down, ears relaxed and down, a relaxed facial expression, and rhythmic contraction of his hind leg muscles. His heart rate and breathing increase. He then relaxes on the mare's back and, after a few seconds, she steps forward to let him drop gently to the ground. Stallions can mate many times a day if a mare (or mares) is in full estrus.

DOMESTIC ERRORS

On domestic stud farms, breeding practice is often different from that in the wild, and horses are normally not allowed to court or mate naturally. This can distress them, so conception rates are understandably poor in comparison.

"Leave me alone."

Signs of approaching foaling include softening and sagging of the tissues of the hindquarters and the enlargement of her udder. When foaling is only days away, milk is produced, the mare's belly hangs low, and she may have a waxy substance on the ends of her teats. She may show signs of considerable discomfort now, as her uterus tenses and relaxes in preparation for foaling contractions. She may be slightly constipated and her legs may swell. Her cervix, vagina, and vulva relax to assist birth, and the mare may become irritable or nervous, have difficulty passing droppings, and may perform flehmen, perhaps as a sign of discomfort. She may lie down more or, because it is uncomfortable, may not lie down at all. She may actually have mild colic, kicking at her belly, looking around at it, and perspiring or even groaning. When foaling is imminent, the udder will have "bagged up," being full of colostrum. The fetus will have turned into its birth position, and the root of the mare's tail and flanks will be loose and sunken. The mare will start seeking private areas a little away from the herd, not wanting to interact with people or other animals.

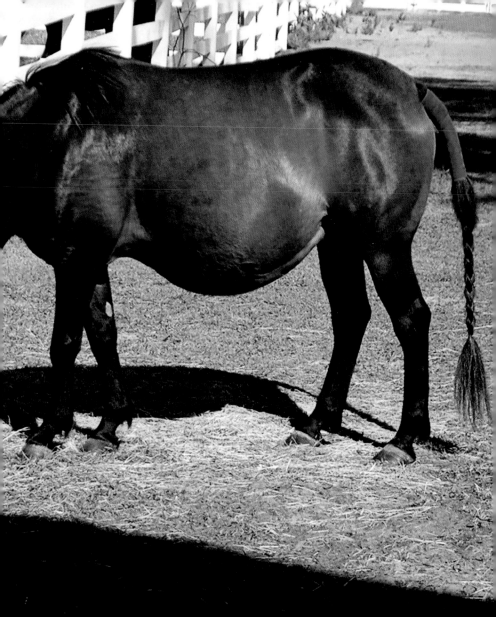

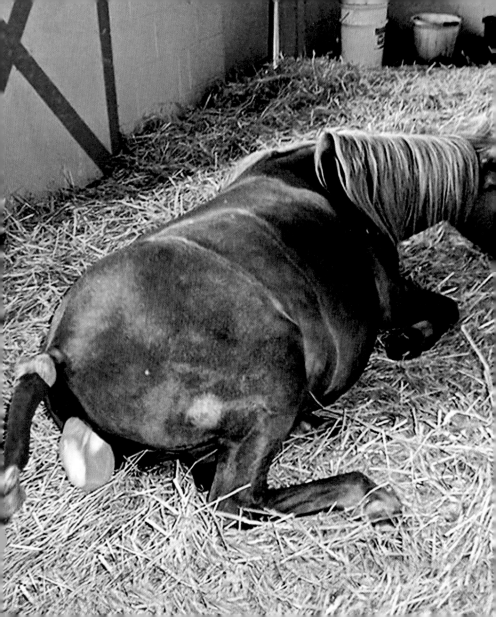

"Don't try watching. I'll only wait until you've gone."

Most mares prefer to foal in privacy and darkness. In the early stages, they can even postpone foaling until they feel safe. The mare will have had painful contractions for about an hour before birth and have been nervous, restless, and may be sweating and running milk from her teats. This stage of labor can actually last from minutes to weeks, coming and going. The mare usually lies down for actual foaling. Strong uterine contractions will cause the mare to strain and push with her belly muscles, holding her breath for extra force. The foal's forefeet will break the placenta, the inner membrane inside the uterus which has serviced his development up to now, and the mare's waters break, the fluid between the uterus wall and the placenta flowing out of the vulva. She may lie down and get up several times, but will almost always foal lying down. The foal should come out with one foreleg slightly in front of the other with the head on the knees. Over minutes, more contractions gradually push the foal out until he is resting with his hind legs inside the mare's vagina.

"Let us bond."

The membrane over the foal's nose should break and he will splutter and gasp for air as he learns to breathe in this cold and strange new world. The mare may turn up onto her breastbone and look around at her foal—a point at which many amateur breeders become tearful! She will smell and lick her foal all over to dry him and learn his unique smell. A few more contractions push out the hind legs. Mare and foal remain lying down to rest (in domestic conditions, they should be left in peace to do this). It is best to let the umbilical cord break and seal on its own. The mare may whicker to her foal and show great interest in him. After about forty-five minutes, the mare will stand up, as the afterbirth will be expelled before long—a process known as "cleansing." It will hang down for some hours and the mare runs the risk of a torn uterus if she treads on it. On stud farms, it is usually tied up for this reason.

THE ROLE OF HUMANS

On domestic studs, some people are far too keen to interfere with the whole process. They should stay away, looking on via closed-circuit television or discreet peepholes to check on the progress, interfering only if things are obviously going wrong or to tie up the afterbirth.

"I've got free milk on tap."

It may take a foal about half an hour to stand up, rockily at first, but he will quickly and instinctively learn. Feral foals need to be able to run with the herd after only three or four hours. The first milk, or colostrum, is crucial to the foal's immunity from disease, so his first instinct, after falling all over the place trying to stand up, will be to find the udder. This may take an hour or two. The foal is attracted to any dark corner, so experienced mares position themselves to try to ensure that this dark corner is their udder. They relax the hind leg away from him to tilt the udder toward him and may guide the foal with their muzzle until he finally locks onto a teat, instinctively suckling, which stimulates the letdown and production of milk. A newborn foal should suckle for a minute or so several times an hour. As days and weeks go by, he will suckle for longer but less often.

VITAL COLOSTRUM

The foal's gut is only capable of absorbing protective antibodies for a maximum of forty-eight hours, but its ability to do this decreases from six hours of age onward. This is why it is crucial for the foal to learn to suckle as soon as possible.

"I want my mommy!"

In the wild, the loss of a foal's dam means death to the foal, as other mares will not suckle a foal who is not their own. He will die of starvation or, most likely, predation. In domesticity, however, it is possible for an orphan or rejected foal to be adopted by a bereaved mare. Her own dead foal may be skinned and the skin placed over the orphan so that he will smell like her foal. The pair are carefully introduced by experienced handlers and one will usually have to stay with them around the clock to prevent the foster dam from savaging or even killing the foal. If they have bonded well, things should progress smoothly. The orphan needs colostrum, so if the foster dam cannot be suckled yet, he will need some from other mares on the stud farm or in the surrounding region, if necessary. Special colostrum formula can be obtained from veterinarians or private services and should be kept on hand in case there is such an emergency.

"I might be a burden, but I'm cute."

Rearing foals by hand is a poor alternative to adoption, especially because the foal must socialize naturally with other horses to ensure that it thinks and behaves like a horse when it is older. It is also extremely time-consuming for his attendants, as bottle-feeding special mare-formula milk must initially be done every hour around the clock. Never turn an orphan out alone with other mares and foals, as it will be completely ostracized, kicked around, and may even be killed. Try to find a kind "nanny" mare for company if a foster dam cannot be found.

"Are you mine?"

Mares do not take naturally to other mares' foals, so a bereaved mare can be a particularly sad sight. Her pain can be relieved by adopting an orphaned or rejected foal from another mare (see previous page) but she must be persuaded by humans to do this. Bereaved mares can be so devastated that they become savage and violent, even though they normally have the sweetest natures. A mild sedative may be administered, on the advice of a veterinarian, to help her during this process, and through that of adopting a bereaved foal. If her foal died around birth, some of her waters can be smeared on a prospective adoptee (who can be any age so long as he is still suckling) and the skin of her foal draped on him for her to smell, in hopes that the scent will cause her to think that the foal is hers. The process is usually successful, but not always.

NOT "MOM" MATERIAL

Some mares are just not cut out for motherhood. These are the ones whose response to their foals range from pushing them away from the udder and themselves, to savage biting, kicking, and even trying to kill them. Such foals should be removed and treated as orphans and the mares not be bred from, as it seems likely that the condition is inherited.

"Time to meet the neighbors."

Naturally born foals may be kept a little apart from the herd by their dams for a few days, but eventually the dam will escort her new arrival to the herd to introduce him. In stable herds, the family might approach during birth (they will know if they are not wanted) and show great interest in the foal. On domestic studs, if the mare foals indoors, they can go out into a manure-free small nursery paddock for a couple of hours or so, provided that it is warm and dry. Both of them will adjust more to their new situations if they can be out in good conditions. The foal will keep trying out his long legs and frolicking around. Fine-skinned and fine-coated animals such as thoroughbreds, Arabians, and their crosses should not be out in cool, windy, or damp weather, as they will just stand and shiver, and the foal can become seriously chilled. Breeds with thicker skins and coats—such as native ponies, cobs, and heavy types—can go out in moderate conditions. In nature, horses do not foal in midwinter.

MARAUDING MARES

For several days, it is important that newly foaled mares and foals are kept away from other mares and foals, particularly those they do not know. Mares may be just too inquisitive and a dangerous confrontation can break out. Also, mares without foals may try to steal a youngster from his dam.

"I'm showing my baby."

Watching a mare introduce her foal to the herd can be both a heart-warming and hair-raising experience. The mare will walk ahead and approach the others, maybe at first standing partly between her foal and the new family. There may be ears back, a swishing tail, and a warning look for any member who comes too close. The foal instinctively stays behind Mom, who—by her cross face and possibly bite threats—will fend off overly enthusiastic inquirers. In a feral herd, introductions usually cause no real trouble, but in domestic situations trouble can arise, especially in too-small communal paddocks and/or where strangers are present, such as on a public stud accepting outside mares. On stud farms, competent people must stay to observe and watch carefully for as long as necessary to check that the new additions' companions are safe to be with. If a newly foaled pair is hassled and frightened, with everyone running about too much, they should be removed and placed alone or put with a less-hyper herd—but, again, watched carefully.

"It's best to take things slowly."

Natural weaning is an extremely gradual process. As summer wears on, the foal takes more grass and less milk until, in the fall, he will take an insignificant amount of milk. He will also spend less time with his dam. Lactation is expensive in energy and nourishment for the dam, so her milk supply dries up to help conserve her energy for winter. She may also be pregnant again. She will probably stop her foal from feeding but will allow him to stay around for comfort and companionship. In domesticity, this is rarely allowed to happen. Foals are sometimes abruptly separated from their dams at the too-early age of six months, which is usually very distressing for mares and foals. There are much more gradual methods of weaning, such as waiting until the best-developed foals are at least eight months old before introducing into the herd quiet "nanny" mares with no foals. The dams of these foals are removed and need to be located out of earshot of each other.

"I can't take much more of this."

Occasionally, dams and foals have to be separated for the sake of one or both of them. Some dams are not good mothers, not offering their foals any comfort, maybe not producing enough milk, and not even protecting them from bullying members of the herd, such as other foals. Also, some foals harass their dams mercilessly, constantly biting and butting the udder, playing roughly with their dams, and giving them no peace. In these cases, they obviously need separating. The mare may well not need to be treated like a bereaved mare, but she should be watched carefully to check how she feels. If she appears to be dull and pining, or restless, not eating, or calling for her foal, perhaps she could be a foster dam for an orphan. In any case, she should be put with a good friend or quiet pony, preferably out of earshot of her foal. The foal needs equine company and could be put with a nanny mare or a quiet pony, and bottle-fed if he is still suckling. He may call for his dam and might run up and down looking for her, and, as mentioned, the two should be out of earshot of each other.

"All foals together."

A common system of weaning on domestic stud farms is to put all foals together, or at least in pairs, with no adult company. This is completely unnatural and some researchers and breeders feel sure that it causes behavioral problems later in life, as it is known to do in other species. "Peer grouping," as it is called, regardless of the numbers involved, usually results in one or more of the foals coming out "top dog" in rank, and bullying others with teeth and feet. This creates older horses who, if they have been the bullies, can be difficult for humans to handle. If they were the victims, they can have learning difficulties and a general lack of confidence, often failing to thrive. As they mature, yearlings are usually separated into sex groups as well, and this certainly happens by the time animals are two years old to prevent premature attempts at breeding. The best course of action is always to arrange for one or two quiet, nonbreeding mares or geldings to act as adult minders and teachers for groups of young horses, if their dams cannot be present.

66

"I was here!"
"And so was I!"

Although horses are not territorial in the traditional sense—making dens or lairs and guarding an area— stallions do pass droppings within a temporary, chosen area and along much-used paths. As herds' areas often overlap in the wild, this is simply to inform the neighbors of their continuing presence. A stallion may also pass his droppings on top of those, or on a urine patch of a mare he is interested in, maybe to disguise the fact that she is in season or to mark her smell as accompanying his. The stallion will pass a dropping, then may turn to smell it before moving off. Another stallion will come along and sniff it, then place his smell on top of it. He will then move forward over the pile for a body's length, raise his tail, and pass his own droppings to cover it. If a mare smells a stallion's manure, she will more likely stale (urinate) where she stands in response, rather than try to cover it.

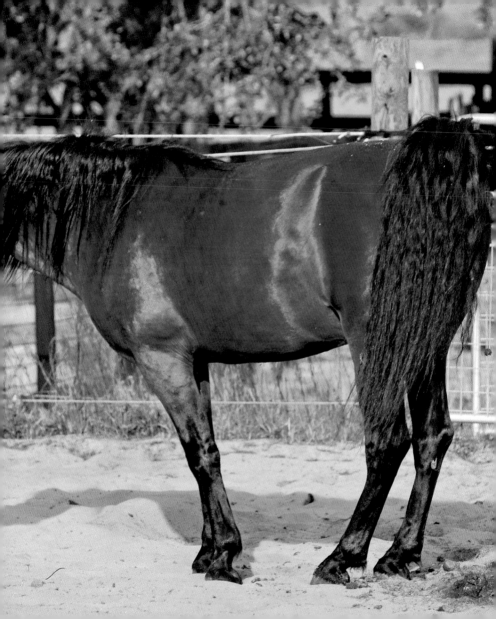

"Who's been here before me?"

When riding out, domestic horses will be interested in any droppings they come across on the trail and will want to stop to identify them, or experience the new smell for their memory bank. They may or may not want to leave their own calling card. Most owners prevent their horses from doing this, which is a great shame because it is important to the horses and takes only a minute.

"Aaaah! That feels good."

Most horses love a good rub and a scratch now and then, and it is part of their way of grooming and relieving an itch. Usually, they rub the crest of the neck and the tail and along the sides. They stand sideways to the chosen tree or post and . . . well . . . just rub themselves up and down and along their bodies. It is thought that because individual horses tend to use the same object, it is a way of depositing their various smells both on the tree or post and on themselves, which combine to create a "herd smell." Horses obviously get a lot of pleasure from rubbing, but it can cause problems if done to excess.

THAT SWEET ITCH

In the skin allergy called "sweet itch," horses are in torment and rub themselves until they are raw and bleeding. Insect repellents and insect-proof sheets, plus constant access to a shelter or stable, are the best ways of prevention, and a vaccine is in development.

"My lovely, lovely horse roll."

One practice that all horses love is to have an energetic roll on a soft surface—or in water, given the chance. The horse will sniff and paw the tempting piece of ground (whether he is being ridden or not!), buckle at the knees, drop onto one shoulder, then rub his side and back on the ground, kicking his legs in the air. A young or agile horse will be able to roll right over and do the other side without having to get up and go down again. On rising, the horse will have a good shake, starting at the front of the body and vibrating right down to the tail. As with rubbing posts, it is thought that horses tend to roll regularly on one or two patches in a paddock to establish a communal herd scent. It is also to help remove dead and loose hair (as horses seem to roll even more when casting their coats). Rolling is extremely important to horses, and they should be given every reasonable opportunity to enjoy it.

"You'd drop, too, if you had to wear these colors."

Many owners complain because their horses either urinate or pass a dropping soon after going into their stable when a clean bed has been put down. They also pass urine and droppings in other horses' stables if they get access to them. This seems certain to be because the horse wants to mark the space as his own, even if he has lived in it for years. As for other horses' stables, this is probably a way of exerting rank over the absent occupant, who is likely to pass a dropping on top of the alien pile when he returns!

EIGHT TIMES A DAY!

Healthy horses pass about eight piles of droppings every twenty-four hours, so there is plenty available for scent-marking stables and small paddocks, and trying to obliterate other horses' droppings passed for the same purpose. Their diet is bulky, so there is plenty of material to pass out of the other end.

"All's right with my world."

You can tell a lot about how a horse is feeling by getting into the habit of watching him closely—his body position, his facial expression, and his behavior. When a horse is feeling settled and content, he will have a soft, relaxed look in his eyes and on his face, a calm air about him, and will be showing interest in his surroundings. His ears will be pricked gently forward at whatever he is currently interested in and his body will feel loose and comfortable to the touch. His tail will softly swing as he moves and will be held loosely down behind his hindquarters.

"That's really frightening!"

The expression of fear is unmistakable after you have had a little experience around horses. Frightened horses usually hold their necks and heads up and back: this is because the head contains the control center for all the senses and is crucial to life. The body will be hard, stiff, and may be trembling and, if he has been frightened for a little while, he may also be showing patchy sweating. He may snort through flared (wide-open) nostrils, and his eyes will be wide with a frightened expression, possibly showing their whites. His muzzle will be tense, with the top lip held out a little over the bottom one. The tail may be held up and out, and will be stiff, or it may be clamped between the buttocks. All his attention will be on what is scaring him and his ears will be pointed hard toward it, wherever it is in relation to his body. He is in no state to listen to his human rider or handler. He is hard-wired by evolution to behave this way.

"I'm angry with you now."

An angry, aggressive horse is a dangerous customer. A horse's strength makes him a formidable enemy to any animal, including humans. An aggressive horse will have an angry expression on his face and in his eyes. His facial skin will be tight, his ears pinned hard and flat back against his neck, and he may be tossing his head at the object of his anger, maybe snapping out at it and half rearing up and down. His tail may be thrashing around. If he is being ridden, he may be kicking out and refusing to go forward willingly.

"Just stay away from me!"

A defensive posture is similar to anger and the two can be felt at the same time. The horse will use his natural weapons—his teeth and feet, front and/or back—to defend himself, along with displaying an angry expression. He may lunge out toward an irritating animal or human with his teeth and may half rear and lash out with his front feet. Mares in particular tend to turn tail and kick out with their hind feet at the person or animal concerned, maybe even running back into them, kicking as they come. Sideways (cow) kicks often catch people by surprise, though other horses are often ready for them. A horse can reach out a surprising distance sideways and forward with a hind foot, even reaching a person standing by its shoulder.

"This is really upsetting me."

It is awful to see a big, strong—yet sensitive—animal like a horse in distress. This emotion is usually experienced when the horse feels trapped and unable to improve his lot, such as when ridden by a harsh rider, but also if turned out in a small area with an aggressive horse. Pain also causes similar signs. In mental distress and anxiety over a situation, the horse will have a tight, hunched-up appearance to his body, his ears will probably be to the side or slightly back, his eyes may be frightened or have a sunken, defeated look, and his muzzle will be tense with his nostrils wrinkled up and back. If ridden, he may produce excessive froth around his mouth and may sweat up. Pain can cause patchy sweating and the horse may look toward the painful area. In colic (abdominal pain) he may kick at his belly. Head pain may be suspected if the horse presses his head against a firm object like a wall or tree. He may also moan.

"Don't hurt me; I'm no threat."

A horse may show a higher-ranking horse or human that he is aware of their status and that he is no threat to them. He'll do this by holding his head out and down toward them, ears softly pointed toward them, and hold his body in a still, slightly drooping demeanor. This is not fear but what we would probably call respect. Youngsters may show it to older horses and sometimes in-season mares to stallions. High-ranking geldings may exhibit the snapping action described earlier—the head is held out and low, and the front teeth are snapped or clapped together quickly a few times. All horses understand this movement, but inexperienced humans usually think that the horse is trying to bite them.

"Stay away; I don't feel very well."

Horses who don't feel well usually keep themselves a little apart from the herd. In a stable they may stand at the back, away from the door (and the world). Their eyes will be dull and may appear sunken, the ears will be loose and back or sideways, and the head will be level with the withers (or lower). They usually show little or no interest in what is going on around them and, depending on their problem, may lie down a lot more. Ironically, they may not lie down at all if it is too uncomfortable to do so. If a horse has been standing in this manner for over an hour, and is not just dozing, you can justifiably suspect sickness or an undetected injury.

"I'm hyped up and ready to explode, so watch out!"

Some horses get excited very easily. These are usually horses of hotblood breeding such as thoroughbreds, Arabians, and their crosses, or horses who have been badly treated in the past. The head and neck will be held up and the body will feel tense, maybe trembling slightly, which is also a sign of apprehension or fear. A feeling of excitement will cause a horse to have widened eyes, flared nostrils, and ears pricked toward the object of the horse's excitement. There will be no look of fear or panic on his face. The horse's tail will be up and rather stiff, and he may snort and cavort around. He may also neigh loudly.

"I'll scratch yours if you'll scratch mine."

Horses both feral and domestic love grooming themselves, along with their family and friends. Self-grooming consists of rubbing to scratch an itch and to remove loose hair, especially in the spring and fall when changing coats. Rolling is a form of self-massage, again to remove hair and, it is believed, to coat the horse in dust or mud, which may help to discourage skin parasites. When mud is plastered on and dried, it can act like a portable shield against wind. Mutual grooming, or allogrooming, is when two horses stand head to tail and—using their front teeth and muzzles—scrape, nuzzle, and lick their partner mainly in the lower neck, withers, and the front of the back area. They obviously get a lot of pleasure out of this. It may be done to strengthen relationships and to make a friend feel good, as it is known to lower the heart rate.

"A little dirt don't hurt!"

Horses usually roll, given the chance, after work when they may have been hot and sweaty, and to give their heads and saddle patches a good rub. They enjoy rolling as self-massage. Nearly all horses also love rolling and pawing in fresh snow, not to mention playing in it, especially if there is a friend or two around as well. The delight they show is glorious to see.

"Kittens aren't the only ones with whiskers."

The coarse whiskers, or vibrissae, around a horse's muzzle (and, to a lesser extent, his eyes) are special feeler whiskers, which are important to him for feeling objects close to his head that he cannot see clearly, especially in the dark. For this reason, they should never be clipped off, even though some feel that horses look "neater" without them. This is often done when horses are being tidied up for a public occasion, but is now banned by several showing organizations and breed societies. It is actually illegal in Germany. Some horses refuse to eat when their whiskers are clipped off, and may also bang their heads if their eye whiskers are removed. They do adapt, but it is not a horse-friendly thing to do.

"Why must you do these things to me?"

Horses who are afraid of veterinarians, equine dentists, and farriers are not uncommon. These skilled professionals are needed to maintain a horse's health. Horses need vaccinations and may become sick or injured. Their teeth and mouths must be in good condition for efficient chewing and to take a bit, and farriers will be needed to trim a horse's feet expertly, even if he is not shod. Unfortunately, despite being professionals, some people are rather rough with horses, and veterinary attention by its very nature can feel uncomfortable or painful. Some farriers are prone to being rough and hurried with horses, which is not pleasing to a horse. Farriers may also hold up the horse's legs too high and bring them too far out to the sides; this overstresses the joints and can be painful, especially when the horse is not allowed any relief for extended periods. The solution is to tell the person treating your horse about the horse's fear and ask for his or her cooperation. Try to get your horse accustomed, as best you can, to accepting actions similar to those the handler will carry out, and give your horse plenty of tidbits so that he will associate treatment with enjoyment.

"I feel so much better after a really good chew."

The lifestyles of many horses are so unnatural and stressful to them that they are pushed into starting to perform what used to be called "stable vices" but are now called "stereotypical behavior patterns" or "stereotypies," as also seen in disturbed humans and zoo animals. The most common are: cribbing, where the horse grips a firm object with his teeth, such as a manger or door, and makes a grunting noise; wind-sucking, which is similar but the horse does not need to grip anything; weaving, where the horse sways his forehand, head, and neck from side to side; box-walking, where the horse tramps continually around and around his stable; wood-chewing, which is self-explanatory; head-twirling, where the horse twirls and tosses his head for no apparent reason; and scraping the teeth over the door, where the horse scrapes a crescent-shaped line on the outside of his stable door with his front teeth. Improving the horse's lifestyle helps, but no vice has been completely cured by nonsurgical means once it has become established. Contrary to general opinion, horses do not "catch" stereotypies from each other, and it is now considered best to allow the horse to perform his particular action because of the relief it gives him.

84

"I just can't go on any longer."

Because many horses are used by humans for athletic pursuits, they are sometimes pushed to their physical limits and should be made fully, athletically fit before being asked to work hard. Even so, horses can become exhausted both mentally and physically. The signs of physical exhaustion are sweating (sometimes heavy), a distressed look on the horse's face, staggering, inability to work due to extreme lack of energy, and maybe even collapse. Signs of mental exhaustion can be a total lack of interest in anything or, conversely, aggression. The performance of a stereotypie, dullness, an air of resignation, or the lack of a previous level of ability in a sport are also indicative. Being sensitive to a horse's normal character and being suspicious when it changes is always a good way to keep track of how a horse is coping with his life.

"I'm much taller than you."

Playing horses—almost always colts and geldings, but often stallions as well—love to rear up as part of their games. This is practicing for stallion behavior and fighting off a rival in the wild, but domestic horses clearly enjoy the sensation, too. The horse will stop and lift up his forehand, standing on his hind legs in a half or full rear, maybe also waving his forelegs about. His play partner will probably do the same.

"Here's how much this hurts!"

When rearing occurs under saddle (other than on command in display riding), it is extremely dangerous, as the horse can easily overbalance and come over backward on top of his rider. In such cases, it is usually caused by mouth pain from the teeth or a harshly used bit. The rider should sit forward and hold the mane, and be very still, loosening the reins, so as to give the horse the ability to balance. As soon as he comes down, walk or trot him on briskly with a loose rein.

"I feel absolutely terrific!"

Horses play-buck most often when playing alone. They may do it in company, too. They put their heads and necks down and jump up into the air off all fours, maybe repeating it several times, or they will alternately kick up and down with their front and back legs, moving along as they go. They clearly enjoy it and it uses up lots of energy; it is also an expression of equine joy.

THE BUCK STOPS HERE

Under saddle, bucking can be frightening and dangerous. Any horse can buck off almost any rider if he really wants to, usually because his back is hurting from injury or a badly fitting saddle. Sometimes it's because the rider is asking him to do something he does not want to do. Once a horse has deposited a rider with a good buck, he knows forever that this is possible and may resort to it whenever he does not want to work. Keeping the horse moving forward at a brisk pace and not letting him get his head down when in motion is a good preventive to bucking. The latest theory, however, is to stop the horse and make him stand still for several seconds to break the expression of the flight-or-fight response, which is enhanced by speed.

"Around and around we go."

When playing, horses often run rings around each other—all the while biting, play-kicking, and barging as they go. They will also try to get a foreleg over their partner's neck in an act of dominance. This is all good practice for when they are in charge of a herd and have to fend off intruders and usurpers, even though it is never going to happen. Stallions often bite each other's legs, trying to bring down their opponent. Then, in the wild, they might disembowel him with their teeth, but domestic play rarely gets this far, as there is not normally anything to actually fight over. Mares also play, of course, but more with mock kicking, running side-by-side, tossing their heads, bucking, and frolicking—much more ladylike. Foals play most of all, using all these techniques, and all horses will play alone if they have no companion.

"I'm a coiled spring waiting to go off."

There is a special arrangement of ligaments and joints in a horse's legs that let him lock them into place without conscious effort, which allows him to sleep lightly standing up. This is called the "stay mechanism" and is a brilliant survival device to enable a horse to be running with the herd within a second or two of receiving a warning of a predator. It is also used to good effect by horses who dare not lie down to sleep. This can happen after moving yards when they still feel insecure, in a too-small stable, or if they have a weakness or physical pain, which makes lying down and getting up difficult and painful. Horses can go for years without lying down, but it is not a good way to live, and everything should be done to ascertain the cause of it and put it right.

"Zero to full gallop: three seconds flat."

Often, a horse will get down on the ground but not lie flat out on his side. He will prop up on his breastbone like a dog, and can sleep very well in this position. As he is partly up, he can, if necessary, quickly raise his forehand on to his front feet, lurch his hindquarters up with a thrust from his hind legs, and be up and running in about three seconds.

STUCK IN THE MIDDLE

If ever you see a horse sitting on his hindquarters like a dog, clearly trying to get up but without success, and maybe swiveling around on his bottom as he does so, it is a sign of considerable weakness or pain in his hindquarters or hind legs. A sound, healthy horse can be on his feet in a few seconds, so if yours cannot do so, he needs veterinary attention quickly, as he can break bones or suffer serious muscle injuries in his struggles.

9

"I'm lost to the world."

Horses experience their deepest sleep when lying flat out on their sides. It is in this state that they dream, and their eyes and muzzles and legs can be seen twitching. It is actually possible to go right up to a horse in this state without waking him up (although it is not recommended, in case he does so and panics), and therefore it is a very dangerous position and state for him to allow himself to go into. In wild and feral conditions, the herd guards, described earlier, give warning of intruders, but it takes a horse lying flat out and sleeping deeply the longest time of all to get to his feet and galloping. Horses will not do this if they do not feel completely secure and free to get up, and they only stay in this position for half an hour at most.

A GOOD NIGHT'S SLEEP? HMMM.

Horses do not sleep all through the night as we do. They sleep about half an hour at a time, waking and walking around eating, then lying down again. This is a survival mechanism, and is also the reason why the bedding in their stables is often in such a turmoil in the mornings, and why all their food is gone. Horses are most active around dawn and dusk, tending to sleep, rest, and relax in the middle of the day and night, given the choice. It is easy to see how a domestic lifestyle disrupts what nature intended for them.

"Is there anybody out there?"

The most familiar sound people associate with horses is the neigh. This is an instantly recognizable, loud noise that horses use to call to others. His head will be up, his ears forward, and his body vibrates all over as he neighs. When people are out with their horse, it can be annoying when he constantly neighs and pays little attention to his rider. This shows that he is anxious for supportive equine company and is not satisfied with that provided by his rider. The answer is to do all you can to become strong, positive, calm, and trustworthy, and to improve your relationship.

"It's so good to see you again."

A whinny is similar to a neigh but is less urgent in quality, softer, and is done to a familiar horse or person, or to another animal in greeting. It is one of the most heartwarming things a horse can do for a caring owner, to welcome her in this way, especially if she never carries tidbits and the horse is clearly welcoming her for herself.

"I love you."

The nicker (or whicker) is an intimate sound horses make to close friends and family, a mare to her foal, a closely bonded stallion and mare to each other, or a horse to a favorite rider. This is a low, very personal sound made to a person or animal close by and highly regarded, welcomed into the horse's space and whose presence gives the horse pleasure. As the object of the whicker will be close by, the horse's head will be lowered and there will be a soft look in the eyes. It is a low, vibrating sound, breathy and confidential, recognized by all horses and caring horse people.

"I've got a bad feeling about this."

When horses squeal, it is usually because they are cross, indicating aggression and threats. When two nonfriendly horses meet, there is almost always a deal of squealing, maybe stamping with a forefoot and even a swing around of the hindquarters with a threat of kicking. Horses rarely squeal at humans, unless the human hurts them. Usually, there is a cross facial expression, nostrils wrinkled up, a tense muzzle, and face and ears pointing toward wherever the unwelcome horse happens to be.

"I think I'm hungry again."

Because horses in natural conditions always have food available, domestic ones need a supply of food nearly all the time. They can become uncomfortable and anxious when they are deprived of food for several hours. Hunger is unnatural for horses and makes them restless, tense, and discontented. It is also known to predispose them to gastric ulcers. If they are prone to a stereotypical behavior, they will almost certainly perform it when hungry. The best way of preventing this unhealthy situation is to simply make sure that the horse always has food available when he is not working—either a field in which to graze or a full hay container. If your horse or pony needs his diet to be rationed due to a tendency towards obesity or laminitis, give him low-calorie food specially designed for his type, so that he can eat adequately and not be hungry, yet still avoid the dangers of overeating.

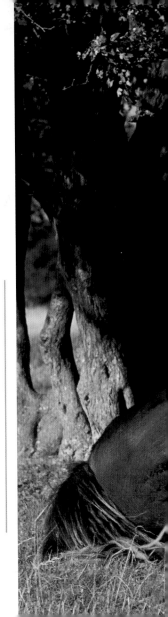

"Back off! This is my patch."

When horses live outside and are fed together, trouble can arise unless the situation is managed properly. Extra feeds might be needed when the grazing is poor or overeaten, which can cause skirmishes. It can even happen when a horse wants to protect a particular piece of grazing. All the usual signs of aggression will be present as the higher-ranking horse chases off the underling from his rations: ears back, bite threats, or actual bites and nips. In the case of a high-ranking horse, a warning look that plainly says, "Back off!" might be all that's needed. It is safest to space apart feed bowls and buckets at least twenty to thirty feet, or even more if trouble is expected. Ideally, the lower-ranking horses should be brought out of the field and fed where others cannot get to them.

"There's plenty for everyone."

Feeding fibrous roughage such as hay or haylage in the field is often necessary and, to ensure that every horse can have a share, there must be at least one more pile or net than there are horses. This way, when they swap around—as they do—there is always somewhere for the underlings to go. If hay is fed from one large, communal container, low-ranking horses may be frightened to approach and get their share, so this situation must be watched for, and extra supplies put out for them.

"There's nothing like a cool drink on a hot day."

When having a long drink, a horse will take several swallows, then raise his head to look around for predators, and then have a break—yet another evolutionary behavioral pattern that has remained with modern horses. Then he will usually drop his head and drink some more, moving away from the source of his own accord when he has had enough.

GIVE HIM TIME TO DRINK HIS FILL

In the past, it was considered necessary to take horses to water two or three times a day, let them drink their fill, and then return them to their fields and stables. With modern plumbing for paddocks and stables, this is rarely necessary, although it may be practiced with working horses out on long days. It is now recommended that horses have water available more or less all the time, so that they can drink as they need to—and they need roughly ten or twelve gallons each day depending on workload and weather. Another old, inaccurate idea was that horses should not be allowed to drink during and just after feeding. We now know that moderate drinks at these times actually help digestion. Horses' natural food—grass—is moist, with a high water content.

"I'm one cool dude."

A horse's normal body temperature is about 100.4°F and, as a mammal, it is capable of maintaining its body temperature internally, except in extreme weather. One of the best ways to help him do this is to ensure that he always has access to a good shelter that protects him from cold winds, rain, and wet snow in winter and hot, dry sun in summer. Do not leave him standing around in cold, windy, wet conditions without a blanket or shelter, especially if he is clipped. In hot, especially humid weather, keep him in the shade when not working; do not blanket him and do not work him hard and fast.

REACTING TO THE WEATHER

Horses stand with their tails to the wind and rain, and always seek shade when the sun is hot. A horse suffering from hypothermia (too cold) or hyperthermia (too hot) will be dull, lethargic, and miserable. A cold horse may well shiver and a hot one may pant and sweat. Allowing the body temperature to move significantly above or below normal is dangerous and possibly lethal, so their reactions to weather must be watched and their temperatures monitored.

Index

Acknowledgments

Books are always a team effort and there are more people involved in them than readers will ever know. I wish to thank Horsepix for their professional expertise in taking and providing most of the photographs, which are such an essential part of this book. Every author is always aware that one picture is worth a thousand words and that illustrations can make or break any publication.

I should like to thank all the staff at Anova Books and everyone who took the time and trouble to be available for the photography.

Unless stated, all pictures from Horsepix Equestrian Photography, www.horsepix.co.uk, with the exception of:

Rebekah Rodger: Page 7.
Anova Image Library: Pages 5, 11, 14, 22, 24, 26, 29, 30, 34, 37, 41, 47, 49, 53, 69, 75, 199.
Photos Cheval: Pages 8, 12, 16, 38, 42, 44, 71, 72.